American History: The United State [federal] republic composed of 50 s[tates,] [a] district, five major self-governing territories, and various possessions. At 3.8 million square miles and with over 325 million people, the United States is the world's third- or fourth-largest country by total area and the third-most populous. The capital is Washington, D.C.

## Famous Civil Rights Quotes:

**"It is impossible to struggle for civil rights, equal rights for blacks, without including whites. Because equal rights, fair play, justice, are all like the air: we all have it, or none of us has it. That is the truth of it."**
Dr. Maya Angelou

**"Darkness cannot drive out darkness; only light can do that. Hate cannot drive out hate; only love can do that."**
Reverend Dr. Martin Luther King, Jr.

# Special Thanks

This book is a brief biography of Erlene Menzella Rucker Crosslin and her legal battle for employment in America. Special thanks to my many family and friends who contributed to this effort. Their contributions are remembered in the Appendix of this book under Acknowledgements.

# Crossing Over on the Shoulders of Giants
# American History Biography
# of the
# 1964 Title VII Civil Rights Act Champion

## Erlene Menzella Rucker Crosslin

*To Erlene's credit, she discovered how to continue the legal fight for civil rights for all Americans. She lived everyday knowing that "the nonviolent fight for civil rights continues".*

---

By Gloria Crosslin, DHA, Doctor of Health Administration

# DEDICATION

Erlene Menzella Rucker Crosslin is noted for her belief that every American should have the right to equal employment without fear of discrimination or reprisal.

In 1970, Erlene Crosslin won the legal battle to eliminate employment discrimination. The Supreme Court agreed with Erlene and her case sets precedence that employment should not be dependent upon a person's race, disability or religion.

Erlene accomplished this great feat by crossing over on the shoulders of civil rights giants. Many are given credit throughout this book. People not mentioned are still remembered in the hearts of those who knew their struggles.

# PURPOSE

The purpose of this book is to experience American history through the life of Erlene Menzella Rucker Crosslin.

Erlene's contribution to American history was truly a sacrifice. This book is an easy read that families can sit down together and discuss.

The book's aim is to inform the reader about employment discrimination during the Civil Rights Movement.

This book can be read in accordance with other American History books.

As an added bonus, a fun workbook is also included.

# PREFACE

The United States of America is well known for its fight for Civil Rights. Before her passing, Erlene Menzella Rucker Crosslin crossed over on the shoulders of giants. She was an honorary lifetime member of the National Association for the Advancement of Colored People. During this long struggle, one of the legal battles fought by the NAACP was to lobby against segregated education.

In 1950, the NAACP formulated a legal strategy against segregated education. This was known as the Freedom Civil Rights Era from 1950–1963.

In 1954, the Supreme Court's landmark Brown v. Board of Education decision allowed African Americans the right to study alongside their white peers in primary and secondary schools.

The decision fueled an intransigent, violent resistance during which Southern states used a variety of tactics to evade the law.

Erlene Menzella Rucker Crosslin began her own personal legal battles for equal employment when she applied for a job. Her well known Supreme Court landmark decision is "Crosslin v. Mountain Bell Telephone and Telegraph."

Readers will come to understand how employment discrimination was applied in Mrs. Crosslin's case. She fought to end employment discrimination because it is a violation of every American's civil rights.

# Table of Contents

# "Crossing Over on the Shoulders of Giants"
# American History Biography
# of the
# 1964 Title VII Civil Rights Act
# Champion
# Erlene Menzella Rucker Crosslin

Erlene Crosslin was a real-life champion of Civil Rights. She was the first African American woman to file and ultimately win a landmark Supreme Court Decision focused on employment discrimination.

The lawsuit was filed against Mountain Bell Telephone and Telegraph Company. Her legal case sets precedence in outlawing discrimination in nearly every facet of American life and makes employment fair and equitable for all Americans.

Erlene is absolutely the missing link between Dr. Martin Luther King, Jr.'s nonviolent legal battle for the civil rights of all Americans. They both believed that every person should be allowed gainful and meaningful status in the workplace. Dr. King marched for equal rights, but it was Erlene who picked up the baton and won the legal rights for all Americans access to equal employment.

After King's death, the movement called Civil Rights Era declined, but not without a nonviolent fight. Erlene knew that she had to continue the legal battle. Her Supreme Landmark Case is a testament to her being a fierce contributor to how Dr. King also lived his nonviolent legal life.

We are proud of Erlene's accomplishments, because she fought passionately and legally for the civil rights of Americans to have equal access to employment.

Many Civil Rights icons were the first to march, sit in, boycott and organize African Americans to fight for civil rights. They were inventors, media, educators, medical personnel, politicians, musicians, ministers, veterans, writers, attorneys, and many other Americans who believed in equal employment. Many are memorialized for their accomplishments.

Unfortunately, many lost their lives for what they believed in, yet these are the giants that helped Erlene solidify legal rights of Americans to obtain work without fear of discrimination and retaliation.

Photo 2: Erlene Menzella Rucker Crosslin

# Introduction

In 1935, Erlene Menzella Rucker is born in Slate Shoals, Texas to Fannie Mae Bagley (Native American Choctaw Indian) and Lawyer Rucker (African American/French Canadian) decent.

Photo 3
Lawyer Rucker

Photo 4
Fannie Mae Bagley Rucker

During this time in history it was not uncommon to work extremely hard to maintain life in America.

Slate Shoals was no different than most counties in Texas. Unfortunately, it now has an extinct population due to departure to the original habitants and those who required better opportunities.

Photo 5

Slate Shoals, Texas is located in Lamar County, North Central Texas, FM 906 at the intersection of Springhill Road, just south of the Red River at the Texas State Line, about 6 Miles E of Arthur City, about 15 Miles NE of Paris, Texas.

Photo 6

Although no population figures are available for this tiny place, it did have a school, church and even a factory at one time. It was named for the deposits of slate along the Red River at this point – and most probably the factory was engaged in making roofing shingles.

Photo 7

Although there is no town center and the community dispersed, the name continues to be used on maps.

# Chapter 1: Early Years

Erlene Menzella Rucker was born in a time when American life was desperately difficult for minorities. In 1935, America was dealing with the Great Depression and inching its way towards World War II. In July, of her birth The National Labor Relations Act became law.

The civil climate at that time was very scary. Respectively, other such notable memories include historical facts about Mary McLeod Bethune.

The Great Depression of the 1930s worsened the already bleak economic situation for African Americans. They were the first to be laid off from jobs, and they suffered from an unemployment rate two to three times that of whites.

In early public assistance programs African Americans often received substantially less aid than whites, and some charitable organizations even excluded blacks from their soup kitchens.

Photo 8

While being raised in Texas, Erlene was referred to by family members and close friends as Menzella, her middle name. Her earliest memories most likely were of the challenges she faced trying to survive in a hostile civil climate.

During the same time, the U.S. Supreme Court ruled in the Norris v. Alabama case that a defendant must have the right to a trial by jury by his/her peers.

This ruling overturns the conviction of the well-known case Scottsboro Boys. Also, at the same time of Erlene's birth, Mary McLeod Bethune establishes the National Council of Negro Women--calling more than 20 leaders of national women's organizations together.

Even during the heated civil climate, Erlene recalled happy times and memories of being raised in the Methodist Episcopal Church. The Methodist Episcopal Church was the oldest and largest Methodist denomination in the United States from its founding in 1784 until 1939.

It was also the first religious denomination in the US to organize itself on a national basis, but it no longer exists as the MEC.

While her dad was the most upstanding Deacon that could ever be, with his wife Fannie Mae right there by his side, they made the transition to Baptist.

Erlene's mom, Sister Fannie Mae was a spiritual gospel singer and her favorite song that all churches called upon her to sing every single time she was in the congregation was "Precious Lord". The congregation would break out in emotion.

This life in the church and the guidance of her parents instilled in Erlene the importance of non-violence.

Erlene, as other minority students, attended a segregated school. Charles Hamilton Houston, the dean of Howard Law

School, later made a field trip to the south and filmed the disparities in the segregated south.

The film was first shown at the 1935 Annual conference of the NAACP.

During Erlene's early education, despite the visual evidence of the disparities in the education system provided for African Americans and Whites, it proved difficult to correct the civil indifferences.

The teachers in the primary schools were hired by the local whites and were often too afraid to risk their livelihoods by bringing legal action against their employers. Some communities were similarly reluctant to risk their schools and their jobs by making waves.

Nevertheless, in 1935, Houston persuaded the Virginia teachers association to fight for equal wages. It established a fund to compensate any plaintiff in a teacher salary case who lost his or her teaching post. They began a legal campaign that would take years to bear fruit (February, 2012 The Walter Right Project is the source note).

# Chapter 2: Childhood

In the 1930's, there were not many opportunities for African Americans to work, however shoe-shine positions and those of porters on Pullman cars (railroad sleeping cars), were available. The Brotherhood of Sleeping Car Porters was a strong union of African-American workers during this time period.

Blacks faced segregation every day and were treated poorly. Lawyer, Erlene's father was resourceful and a very influential man and owned plenty of farm-land. He earned money through hard work and what was passed down to him from his family from fur trading in Canada. He used his money wisely to purchase land.

In America, it was not uncommon for landowners who were less resilient to have their lands taken away by unscrupulous landowners, but not Lawyer.

Photo 9

Lawyer did sell a lot of his land-but as a very smart businessman, he kept land for his family. In fact, a portion of the land he sold was known as Guadalupe, in Arizona, which has been redistricted to be known presently as Ahwatukee.

Photo 10

# Chapter 3: Growing up in America

America was established as the land of the free and home of the brave. Erlene was no exception to that creed and she contributed to society in many ways while growing up in America. She recalls how understanding legal discrimination issues where still a factor, even for a young person.

Little did she know that growing up in America would one-day warrant the pursuit of a legal battle. The picture below depicts present day Ahwatukee, Arizona, where she used to help her dad on his farm.

It is a picture where she would bring her children and other family members after a hard day of work, before traveling back to Phoenix.

Photo 11

# Chapter 4: Adulthood

While Erlene was being reared in Arizona, the Vietnam War happened. One of Erlene's brothers was sent off to fight in the war. She remembered military men showing up at her door explaining that there had been an unfortunate accident in which her brother had been wounded in the war. He did recover and served his tour in the army into retirement. Being ever resilient, he reenlisted and retired a second time from the military with honors.

Photo 12

In 1956, Erlene studied at Arizona State University with a summer semester at Wiley College. The school was featured in the movie The Great Debaters, featuring Denzel Washington. A drama based on the true story of Melvin B. Tolson, a professor at Wiley College Texas.

Erlene earned a Bachelor's degree from Texas College and taught the well-known home economics classes that the government sponsored at the community level.

The government provided produce and hired teachers to train community members how to cook government products such as cheese, beans and rice that could be provided to the communities as sanctioned meals.

Photo 13

# Chapter 5: Employment

In 1960, Erlene applied for a job at the telephone company and is denied employment based on her race.

Photo 14

After careful thought, in 1960, Erlene lodge's a verbal complaint to the telephone company about them denying her employment because she is African American.

This angered the telephone company.

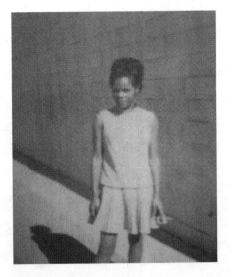

Photo 15

To shut up Erlene, the telephone company handed her a broom and a bucket to position her as a janitor. She was then told to work in the basement.

In the words of Linda Williams, a Fox News Reporter on interview, exclaimed that Erlene said "not so".

As a result of Erlene filing a complaint, the telephone company disconnected Erlene's telephone service in retaliation. But Erlene won her fight for equal employment rights as seen in the photo 16.

Photo 16

# Chapter 6: Legal Battle

1970: Erlene and Robert (husband) file a case against the Telephone Company for racial discrimination and denial of public accommodation.

1970: The United States Supreme Court compels lower courts to hear employment discrimination cases based on Erlene's civil rights.

1971: CROSSLIN v. MOUNTAIN STATES TEL. AND TEL. CO, 400 U.S. 1004 (1971); and 400 U.S. 1004. Erlene CROSSLIN et vir. v. The MOUNTAIN STATES TELEPHONE AND TELEGRAPH CO. is added to law books.

1972: Pacific Maritime Association and International Longshoremen's and Warehousemen's Unions Plaintiff's and appellees cite Crosslin's case as precedence at the United States Courts of Appeal Ninth Circuit.

# Chapter 7: The Battle Continued

1965: White House President Lyndon Baines Johnson invites Crosslin to his second Inauguration Ball.

1978: Crosslin retires from the Arizona State Government Personnel Division Employment System as an EEOC/Personnel Analyst.

1993: Erlene Crosslin is honored with the Martin Luther King "Living the Dream Award" at the America West Arena Ceremony along with Stevie Wonder, respectively the late Rosa Parks and other honorees.

Photo 17

2000: Cornell Law Library, Open Jurist and other legal media outlets add Crosslin v. Mountain Bell to public media access.

2019: International Cancer Advocacy Network (ICAN) celebrate the life and legacy through the Erlene Rucker Crosslin chief program that fight against health disparities.

2020: "Crossing Over on the Shoulders of Giants" is a book written about the civil rights life of Erlene Menzella Rucker Crosslin

Present Day: Erlene Menzella Rucker Crosslin was laid to rest, but her legacy lives on through the hearts of Americans who continue the non-violent fight for Civil Rights

# Credits

**Photos:**

1. Erlene Menzella Rucker Crosslin, book cover
2. Erlene Menzella Rucker Crosslin
3. Lawyer Rucker
4. Fannie Mae Bagley Rucker
5. Photo courtesy Gerald Massey, 2010
6. Photo courtesy Gerald Massey, 2010
7. Photo courtesy Gerald Massey, 2010
8. Library of Congress, Washington, D.C., Arthur Rothstein (neg. no. LC-USF34-005788-D)
9. Farmland in Texas 1930's, Bing.com
10. Guadalupe Arizona Pig Farms 1930's, Bing.com.
11. Ahwatukee Arizona Present Day, Bing.com
12. Staff Sargent JC Rucker with his proud sister, Erlene. His other proud sister is Rosella (of Colorado and the Turner family) and two other brothers, Reverend Billy Rucker (Olive Branch Missionary Baptist Church) and Robert Carl (RC).
13. Home Economics 1950's, Bing.com.
14. Images of Mountain Bell Telephone and Telegraph 1950's, Pininterest.com.
15. Erlene Menzella Rucker Crosslin, early years
16. Erlene Menzella Rucker Crosslin with one of her grandsons who lives in Germany
17. Dr. Martin Luther King, Jr., Dream Award presented to Erlene Crosslin

## Source Notes:

1. Civil Rights Act of 1964. Retrieved from
https://www.loc.gov/exhibits/civil-rights-act/civil-rights-era.html

2. February, 2012 The Walter Right Project is the source note at
http:scalar.usc.edu/nehvectors/stakeman/school-segregation-in-the-1930s

3. Linda Williams, Fox 10 News Reporter, 1993 on interview

## Contact

Dr. Crosslin earned a doctorate of health administration degree from an accredited university. Gloria researched Wellness Program Incentives for employers to benefit employees. You can reach her at gcrosslin@att.net or 202-834-8639.

# Appendix

Acknowledgments are important to solidify a common bond, especially among diverse people from all backgrounds. As a result, a special thanks to all those who participated in the creation of this book.

As a contribution to them, a bonus history workbook has been included for discussion topic ideas. It's a fun activity for adults to share with children and includes *fun facts* and *fun foods* at the end.

# Timeline: Visual Key

Mrs. Erlene Crosslin
Black History Achievement: The Fight for Civil Rights

Mrs. Erlene Crosslin is the first African American woman to file and ultimately win the Landmark Supreme Court Decision of 1964 Title VII Civil Rights Act Employment Discrimination case against Mountain Bell Telephone and Telegraph Company. Her case sets precedence in outlawing discrimination in nearly every facet of American life and to make it more fair and equitable for all Americans.

**Entries above the timeline:**

- **1935:** Born in Pata... (next to Frankie Alice (Choctaw Indian) and Lawyer Rucker (African American/French Canadian))
- **1960:** Mountain Bell denied Erlene employment based on her race
- **1960:** Erlene's telephone service was disconnected in retaliation
- **1965:** White House jurisdiction Crosslin to desegregation Bell
- **1970:** The United States Supreme Court compels lower courts to hear employment discrimination cases based on Erlene's civil rights
- **1972:** Pacific Maritime Association and International Longshoremen's and Warehousemen's Union Plaintiff's and appellees cite Crosslin's case as precedence at the United States Court of Appeal Ninth Circuit
- **1978:** Crosslin retires from the Arizona State Government Personnel Division Employment given by the EEOC/Personnel Analyst
- **2000:** Cornell Law Library, Open Juris and other legal audits outlets add Crosslin v. Mountain Bell to public media access

**Timeline years:** 1935 · 1940 · 1945 · 1950 · 1955 · 1960 · 1965 · 1970 · 1975 · 1980 · 1985 · 1990 · 1995 · 2000 · 2005 · 2010 · 2015 · 2020

**Entries below the timeline:**

- **1956:** Graduate of sorts; College with a Bachelor's degree, studied at Arizona State University and served a summer semester at Wiley College which was featured in the film Great Debaters, starring Denzel Washington.
- **1960:** Erlene lodges a verbal complaint; She was handed a broom and a bucket, then told to work in the basement
- **1970:** Erlene and Robert (husband) file a case against the Telephone Company for racial discrimination and denial of public accommodation
- **1971:** CROSSLIN v. MOUNTAIN STATES TEL AND TEL CO. 499 US 1004 (1971); and 449 US 1004, Erlene CROSSLIN et vir. v. The MOUNTAIN STATES TELEPHONE AND TELEGRAPH CO. is added to law books.
- **1973:** White House invites Crosslin to Civil Rights Event
- **1993:** Erlene Crosslin is honored with the Martin Luther King "Living the Dream Award" at the America West Arena Ceremony along with Stevie Wonder, the late Rosa Parks and other honorees.
- **Present Day:** Erlene begins the non-violent fight for Civil Rights will continue.

# American History Workbook and Answer Key

This workbook is easy to complete. It has three levels to entice the reader to learn about Civil Rights. For the children's feature, the first segment is about Mary McLeod Bethune, Martin Luther King, Jr, Lyndon Baines Johnson, and Erlene Crosslin.

If the adult reader makes it to level two, this segment features Civil Rights legal battles.

Finally, level three is a question about Rosa Parks.

Let's begin…

## Level One
1. Who was Mary McLeod Bethune?
2. Who was Martin Luther King, Jr?
3. What is the name of the 36th US President?
4. Why did Erlene Crosslin believe in Civil Rights?

## Level Two

1. What is the Supreme Court?
2. Who are the International Longshoreman's Union?

## Level Three

1. What was Rosa Parks famous for?

## Answer Key:

Level One

1. Mary (Jane) McLeod Bethune was an American educator, stateswoman, philanthropist, humanitarian, and civil rights activist best known for starting a private school for African-American students in Daytona Beach, Florida and co-founding UNCF on April 25, 1944 with William Trent and Frederick D. Patterson. She attracted donations of time and money and developed the academic school as a college.

It later continued to develop as Bethune-Cookman University. She also was appointed as a national adviser to the president Franklin D. Roosevelt as part of what was known as his Black Cabinet. She was known as "The First Lady of the Struggle" because of her commitment to gain better lives for African Americans.

2. Martin Luther King Jr. was an American Baptist minister and activist who became the most visible spokesperson and leader in the civil rights movement from 1955 until his assassination in 1968.

Born in Atlanta, King is best known for advancing civil rights through nonviolence and civil disobedience, tactics his Christian beliefs and the nonviolent activism of Mahatma Gandhi helped inspire.

3. Lyndon Baines Johnson, often referred to as LBJ, was an American politician who served as the 36th president of the United States from 1963 to 1969.

Formerly the 37th vice president of the United States from 1961 to 1963, he assumed the presidency following the assassination of President John F. Kennedy.

A Democrat from Texas, Johnson also served as a United States Representative and as the Majority Leader in the United States Senate. Johnson is one of only four people who have served in all four federal elected positions.

4. Erlene believes that employment should be fair for all Americans to work without fear of discrimination and reprisal. The nonviolent fight for civil rights still continues.

# Answer Key:

Level Two

1. The Supreme Court of the United States is the highest court in the federal judiciary of the United States. Established pursuant to Article III of the U.S. Constitution in 1789, it has original jurisdiction over a narrow range of cases, including suits between two or more states and those involving ambassadors.

   It also has ultimate appellate jurisdiction over all federal court and state court cases that involve a point of federal constitutional or statutory law.

   The Court has the power of judicial review, the ability to invalidate a statute for violating a provision of the Constitution or an executive act for being unlawful. However, it may act only within the context of a case in an area of law over which it has jurisdiction.

The court may decide cases having political overtones, but it has ruled that it does not have power to decide non justiciable political questions.

2. The International Longshoremen's Association, AFL-CIO is the largest union of maritime workers in North America, representing upwards of 65,000 longshoremen on the Atlantic and Gulf Coasts, Great Lakes, major U.S. rivers, Puerto Rico and Eastern Canada

**Answer Key:**

Level Three

1. Rosa (Louise McCauley) Parks was an American activist in the civil rights movement best known for her pivotal role in the Montgomery bus boycott.

The United States Congress has called her "the first lady of civil rights" and "the mother of the freedom movement".

## Bonus Play x2

### When did Civil Rights become law?

The Civil Rights Act of 1866, 14 Stat. 27–30, enacted April 9, 1866, was the first United States federal law to define citizenship and affirm that all citizens are equally protected by the law.

### How did Civil Rights become law?

Civil Rights Act of 1964 Becomes Law on July 2nd, marking 51 years since the landmark Civil Rights Act of 1964 became law.

Passed by President Lyndon Johnson after being introduced by his predecessor, John F. Kennedy, the law is perhaps the most significant and widely-referred act of civil rights legislation in the history of the U.S.

# Fill in the Blanks

Martin Luther King, Jr. was born on _ _ _
_ _ _ _ 15, 1929 and died April 04, 1968

## Crossword Puzzle

### Down

1

### Across

1

Down
   1. Antonym for unrest

Across
   1. Opposite of left(s)

# Answer Key
## Bonus Play x2

## Fill in the Blanks

Martin Luther King, Jr. was born on J a n u a r y 15, 1929 and died April 04, 1968

# Answer Key
# Crossword Puzzle

**Down**

**Across**

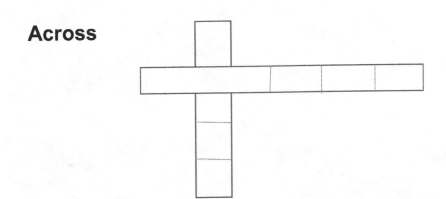

**Down**

CIVIL

**Across**

RIGHTS

# Answer Key
# Crossword Puzzle

```
              C
    R    I    G    H    T    S
              V
              I
              L
```

# Fun Facts

Erlene Menzella Rucker Crosslin
Legendary Civil Rights Champion

## American History: 1964 Title VII Civil Rights Act

Erlene Crosslin was the first African American woman to file and ultimately win the Landmark Supreme Court Decision against Mountain Bell Telephone and Telegraph Company. Her case sets precedence in outlawing discrimination in nearly every facet of American life and to make it more fair and equitable for all Americans.

1935: Erlene is born in Slate Shoals, Texas to Fannie Mae Bagley (Native American Choctaw Indian) and Lawyer Rucker (African American/French Canadian)

1956: Erlene studied at Arizona State University with a summer semester at Prairie View Texas College. She also earns a Bachelor's degree from Texas College.

1960: Erlene is denied employment based on her race.

1960: Erlene lodge's a verbal complaint. She was handed a broom and a bucket, then told to work in the basement.

1960: Erlene's telephone service was disconnected in retaliation.

1965: White House invites Crosslin to Inauguration Ball.

1970: Erlene and Robert (husband) file a case against the Telephone Company for racial discrimination and denial of public accommodation.

1970: The United States Supreme Court compels lower courts to hear employment discrimination cases based on Erlene's civil rights.

1971: CROSSLIN v. MOUNTAIN STATES TEL. AND TEL. CO, 400 U.S. 1004 (1971); and 400 U.S. 1004. Erlene CROSSLIN et vir. v. The

MOUNTAIN STATES TELEPHONE AND TELEGRAPH CO. is added to law books.

1972: Pacific Maritime Association and International Longshoremen's and Warehousemen's Unions Plaintiff's and appellees cite Crosslin's case as precedence at the United States Courts of Appeal Ninth Circuit.

1978: Crosslin retires from the Arizona State Government Personnel Division Employment System as an EEOC/Personnel Analyst.

1993: Erlene Crosslin is honored with the Martin Luther King "Living the Dream Award" at the America West Arena Ceremony along with Stevie Wonder, respectively the late Rosa Parks and other honorees.

2000: Cornell Law Library, Open Jurist and other legal media outlets add Crosslin v. Mountain Bell to public media access.

2019: International Cancer Advocacy Network (ICAN) celebrate the life and legacy through the Erlene Rucker Crosslin chief program that fight against health disparities.

2020: "Crossing Over on the Shoulders of Giants" is a book written about the civil rights life of Erlene Menzella Rucker Crosslin

Present Day: Erlene Menzella Rucker Crosslin was laid to rest, but her legacy lives on through the hearts of Americans who continue the non-violent fight for Civil Rights.

Black History Month Celebration: Olive Branch Missionary Baptist Church, Reverend Billy Wayne Rucker, Pastor and Founder

Contact: Dr. Crosslin, DHA at gcrosslin@att.net

# Sunday Family Dinner Ideas

## <u>Menu</u>

**Fried Chicken Dinner**
**Potato Salad**
**Baked Beans**
**Kale and Collard Greens**
**Apple Pie**

# Menu

**Fish Fry**
**Coleslaw**
**Beverage**
**Lemon Meringue Pie**

# Erlene Menzella Rucker Crosslin
# Book Reviews
# and
# Awards

*This book made a promise to be an easy read and it delivered.*
~ Military Veteran

*Erlene is truly an inspiration for many generations who walk in the footsteps of truth and divine love.*
~Moore Family

*As a nonviolent overcomer, Erlene stands tall teaching us to work hard and make this our best life.*
~Dr. Nannette Williams, Military Veteran and IT Cyber Engineer

*Erlene, you are a legend and thanks for giving me the opportunity to get to know your life story.*
~Dr. Dennis Humphrey, TV Host, International Leadership Author, Lecturer and Road Scholar

*Mom, thanks for this book. You were created to be a star and you are so much more: you were a daughter, sister, Grand mom, Great grandmother, great great grandmother, aunt, cousin, and best friend. We honor you as a Civil Rights icon. In our hearts, you lived a great life to better those before and beyond. Thank you for teaching us about love, dedication and hard work.*
~Crosslin Family


*Erlene Menzella Rucker Crosslin, we salute you for your contribution to America.*
~Rucker Family

*Mother Crosslin, we celebrate your legacy each day and every year.*
~Olive Branch Missionary Baptist Church, Kansas City, Missouri, Reverend Billy Wayne Rucker, Pastor

*I wrote this book through much pain and struggle to educate everyone about the brief life of Erlene Menzella Rucker Crosslin.*
~Gloria Crosslin

## About the Author

In 2011, I earned a doctorate degree in Health Administration.

My picture below is with TV Personality Martha Stewart

My favorite picture is of my mom, sister and myself.